Clay Modelling for Beginners

An Essential Guide to Getting Started in the Art of Sculpting Clay

by Jeanie Hirsch

Table of Contents

Introduction 1

Chapter 1: The Different Types of Clay 7

Chapter 2: Getting to Know Your Clay 13

Chapter 3: Familiarizing Yourself with the Modelling Process 17

Chapter 4: Sculpting Tools Found Around the House 23

Chapter 5: Making a Simple Figure with Oil-Based Clay 29

Chapter 6: Using Advanced Tools for More Complex Projects 33

Conclusion 39

Introduction

Sculpting and modelling with clay is a fun way to spend your spare time. Everyone can enjoy this activity, regardless of age. And the best part is that it doesn't cost much to get started. With a little creativity (and guidance from this book) you can find everything you need already in your home. Yes, there are specialized tools, too, that can make sculpting and modelling with clay easier. However, they are not necessary initially.

This book is designed to help you get started working with clay in a simple, affordable, and fun way by first making small shapes and figures to get familiar with the material and gain practice. Because working with clay is such a relaxing and therapeutic hobby, most people who try it end up completely addicted. Once you come to love the medium, you'll find advice on what additional tools you'll need to invest in to complete projects that are slightly more challenging.

You will also enjoy experimenting with clay extruders, armatures, and larger models. Don't worry if these terms are unfamiliar to you now. This book will cover all the basic terminology, concepts, and materials used, including the various types of clay to choose from. Let's get started!

© Copyright 2015 by Miafn LLC - All rights reserved.

This document is geared towards providing reliable information in regards to the topic and issue covered. The publication is sold with the idea that the publisher is not required to render accounting, officially permitted, or otherwise, qualified services. If advice is necessary, legal or professional, a practiced individual in the profession should be ordered.

- From a Declaration of Principles which was accepted and approved equally by a Committee of the American Bar Association and a Committee of Publishers and Associations.

In no way is it legal to reproduce, duplicate, or transmit any part of this document in either electronic means or in printed format. Recording of this publication is strictly prohibited and any storage of this document is not allowed unless with written permission from the publisher. All rights reserved.

The information provided herein is stated to be truthful and consistent, in that any liability, in terms of inattention or otherwise, by any usage or abuse of any policies, processes, or directions contained within is solely and completely the responsibility of the recipient reader. Under no circumstances will any legal responsibility or blame be held against the publisher for any reparation, damages, or monetary loss due to the information herein, either directly or indirectly.

Respective authors own all copyrights not held by the publisher.

The information herein is offered for informational purposes solely, and is universal as so. The presentation of the information is without contract or any type of guarantee assurance.

The trademarks that are used are without any consent, and the publication of the trademark is without permission or backing by the trademark owner. All trademarks and brands within this book are for clarifying purposes only and are the owned by the owners themselves, not affiliated with this document.

Chapter 1: The Different Types of Clay

There are two main categories of clay, oil-based and water-based. Then there are hybrids and non-clay sculpting materials to consider.

Oil-Based Clays: Oil-based clay is referred to as plasticine. This clay contains oil, sometimes mixed with wax or sulphur. It does not dry out like a water-based clay. Animation artists prefer this clay since the finished pieces can be moved and positions adjusted. Plasticine works well for long-term projects.

Plasticine is good for modelling applications only if it does not contain sulphur. A modelling application means the sculpture will be used to make a mold of the piece. Then multiples will be cast with clay slip, resin, or other materials. The clay piece will then be recycled for another modelling application. If the plasticine contains sulphur, the molding process will not work. So if you intend to make molds of your sculpture, be sure to get plasticine without sulphur.

Plasticine can be purchased from any craft store. It can be found in the children's craft section of major box stores. The best deals for plasticine are usually found on-line at discount stores. A 1 lb. block of plasticine retails for under ten dollars.

Water-Based Clays: These clays are known as ceramic and slip clays. They are clay mixed with minerals and water. They are used for large-scale modelling, creation of ceramics such a dinner ware, and slip casting. Slip casting is a process of pouring liquid clay into a mold to produce a hollow form. That form will dry within the mold. Once it is dry, or set, it will be fired at high temperatures in a kiln and then glazed.

These clays tend to dry rapidly and have to be protected from the air. While working with the clay an artist will continuously mist the piece with water. Once the piece is finished and ready to be dried, it will still be wrapped with a damp towel or paper towels to prevent rapid drying. If the piece dries too rapidly, cracks and breaks can occur.

Although this clay can be reused, it is a messy process if the clay dries out completely. The hardened clay will have to be soaked in a bucket of water and broken down gradually. If the clay has been fired in a kiln, it is not possible to recycle it.

Water-based clay can be purchased from art stores and on-line art stores. A 25 lb. box of clay retails for under 20 dollars. Again, look for great deals from on-line and discount art supply stores.

Paper Clay: Paper Clay is water-based clay with fiber added. Typically paper is the fiber of choice hence the name. This clay is used just like normal water-based clays. The main difference is that unfired pieces are stronger than traditional unfired pieces. It is a good medium for creating dolls.

Paper clay is gaining popularity because it does not require the same attention to detail and joining of pieces. If a crack in the structure occurs, it is easily fixed with a slip made of more paper clay. Details are quickly added onto dry pieces as well. These differences make it a better medium for new artists that wish to make the leap from oil-based to water-based clays.

Paper clay can be purchased from art stores and on-line stores. It can also be made by mixing fibers into water-based clay you may have on hand. Paper clay's retail price varies by application purpose. A 5 lb. bucket of Crayola Air Dry Clay retails for under ten dollars. In contrast, a 5 lb. bag of Activa CelluClay retails at just under 30 dollars.

Polymer Clay: This is not really clay at all. It is a type of plastic made of polymer polyvinyl chloride (PVC) and a liquidizer. This sculpting medium is very firm and requires extensive kneading to become pliable. Once pliable, it is a very easy medium to use. The finished piece can be fired in a kitchen oven at low temperatures. Since a commercial kiln is not needed, polymer clays become more affordable to work with on small-scale projects.

Polymer clay has gained popularity for crafts and figurines. It is also popular for making beads for jewelry applications. It comes in a variety of colors and finishes which reduces the need for painting. It can even be purchased in metallic and pearls.

Polymer clay can be found in most arts and craft stores, box stores, and on-line. The reduced cost in finishing the pieces rounds out the initial cost of the material. Like paper clay, the cost of polymer clay can vary depending on the color and brand. Expect to pay around five dollars per ounce. You can also look for sales on-line.

Now that you are familiar with the types of sculpting and modelling clays, choose the one that you would like to try. Purchase a small amount to practice with first. Then try the exercise in the next chapter.

Chapter 2: Getting to Know Your Clay

Once you choose the clay you want to use, take time to get to know it. Using clay involves all your senses. The smell of clay is very earthy like fresh mud on a rainy day. The clay will feel cool and damp in your hands. Notice the color of the clay and the smooth texture. Listen to the sound the clay makes as you knead it in your hands or on a surface. Listen for any air pockets in the clay to pop. Notice the longer you work with water-based clay the more the air becomes saturated with the dust. You can almost taste the dust as you breathe. Many artists use a dust mask to prevent this from happening, as long-term exposure can be harmful to the lungs.

As you focus your senses on the clay, begin to work it with purpose. Cut off a piece and begin to roll it around in your hands. Take mental notes of how it feels. Is it sticky or smooth? Does it dry out in your hands?

Then flatten the piece out with the palm of your hand. Does it compress easily? Is it stiff like wax or does it become pliable quickly with the heat of your hand. How does it feel to you?

Try pulling the piece apart. Does it come apart like taffy? Do you need a knife because it is dense? Now try rolling a piece between your two hands to make a rope. Once you have the rope, try attaching one end to the other. Does it stick to itself or do you need to moisten the ends with water? If you have chosen a water-based clay, you will need to score both ends and dampen with water before attaching. To score an end you will take a sharp object such as the kabob spear and make multiple X's. Overlap the X's to roughen the section to be pieced together. Dampen the area and then attached the two ends. Use your finger or a tool to smooth the two pieces together.

Next, try making little shapes with the clay. Make a three dimensional rectangle, two triangles, and ball. Place the ball on top of the rectangle at one end. Then put the triangles on the ball, side-by-side. Can you see the start of an animal, perhaps a cat? Now make a tail and legs. Use the end of a paperclip to sketch the face.

Sculpting is really about identifying the shapes in the object you want to copy. Once you have the shapes in mind, figure out their size in relation to each other. For the cat above, the triangles should be much smaller than the ball. The ball will be about one-third the size of the rectangle to be close to the real size of a cat. Since you did not know this was a cat when you started, go ahead and adjust the size of your shapes. Clay is very forgiving and you can rework it as much as necessary.

Continue making shapes and little animals. Then read the next chapter on the process of sculpting and modelling with clay.

Chapter 3: Familiarizing Yourself with the Modelling Process

Working with clay is an exercise in process and patience. There are formal steps to take when sculpting and modelling to ensure the piece will be successful. Patience is needed to take these steps instead of rushing forward to the fun and creative side of detailing your sculpture. The steps below should be used for every sculpture you make. Follow them in order to achieve a successful work of art.

1. **Planning:** Take time to envision the sculpture. What do you want to create? How big will it be? Will it need an armature to hold the weight of the clay? An armature is like a skeleton. It is the framework for the clay so the piece does not collapse. How will you finish the piece?

2. **Sketching:** Sketch or draw your piece from several angles. Draw the basic shapes first. Then add the details you want to capture in the clay piece. Get to know the shapes and angles before you work with the clay. If you are creating a model of an object or person, try sketching from that object or person. If

possible, have that subject present for both sketching and when sculpting.

3. **Measuring:** Measure the object. Decide if you will make a life-sized sculpture or use another ratio. Take the measurements of the object and then convert as needed. For instance, if sculpting a face for a doll from a child, you would want to reduce the measurements by half or more, depending on the doll size. Write all your measurements on your sketch. If possible, have the subject present while sculpting to make additional measurements and conversions.

4. **Armature:** If you will be using large amounts of clay, it is wise to build an armature first. Armatures vary from aluminum foil stick figures to steel pipe frames. Determine how flexible your piece needs to be and how large it will be. The larger the piece, the less flexible, and more sturdy the armature should be. It is good to fill the armature with sturdy materials such as balled up newspaper. Once the armature is packed will fillers, wrap plastic around it and tape it on. The plastic barrier will help keep the clay moist while working on the piece. Using an armature saves clay and reduces your costs in the end.

5. **Building:** Once you have your armature, it is time to start adding clay to the piece. There are many techniques from additive to subtractive sculpting, coiling, and slab building. Your technique will depend on the medium used. There are many books and videos available that teach technique. When you are ready to advance, your local community and art center can also help you with affordable classes.

6. **Symmetry:** When building the initial form, work on symmetry first. If you are working on the doll face, make sure the eyes line up with each other. Look at the placement of all the features and rough them in first. Then measure again to make sure the placement is right. This is the time to make adjustments in the form. It is better to get the form right now, rather than discover you need to move the mouth a half inch after the details have been added.

7. **Detailing:** Once the form has been created and you have confirmed the measurements are right, you can begin adding details. This is the fun part of sculpting. Creating waves in the clothes or hair of the doll is exciting. Let the creative side flow and enjoy the process.

Add enough detail to be interesting. However, be careful not to overwork the piece. Step back from the work every 15 minutes to half hour. Walk around it to see it from all angles. This will give you a fresh perspective and help identify any problem areas.

8. **Finishing:** This will depend greatly on the materials used to create the piece. Drying, firing, baking, glazing, and painting are all options. Creating a mold of the piece to make duplicates can be a fun endeavor for those who like process based applications.

To complete the process above you will need the right tools. Many of which can be found in your house. The next chapter will guide you on how to use these initial tools.

Chapter 4: Sculpting Tools Found Around the House

Before you invest large amounts of money into the tools of the trade, play with clay using tools you have lying around the house. Here is a list of items commonly found in most homes. When you are sure you want to pursue clay formally, you can begin to purchase specialized tools. A list of those tools can be found in Chapter 5.

First, go to your kitchen and look around. Keep in mind though that if you use something for clay, you probably should not use it for food anymore. Exceptions are metal objects that can be cleaned well.

Rolling pins can be used to flatten clay. If your rolling pin is wood, you can wrap it with plastic wrap for the first few uses. That way if you decide you do not like using it, you can still use if for food.

Pasta makers are great for making ribbons of clay. They can also be used to mix polymer clay colors. Only do this if you really like the clay process and will not use the pasta maker for food ever again.

Spoons, knives, forks can all be used for cutting, scoring, and detailing clay.

Meat tenderizers are great for texturing, as are **cheese graters**.

Corn-on-the-cob holders, tooth picks and kabob spears are great for making holes and adding detail.

Aluminum foil, bread ties, paper towel rolls, and paper towels can all be used to create an armature.

Lazy Susan's are great for turning your work to see different angles while working. You do not have one? Take the **spinning glass plate from your microwave**. It works really well too.

Other areas of your house will have useful tools as well. In your home office, you might find the following items:

Paper clips can be used to tie armature or for scoring and making holes.

Scissors are great for cutting clay.

Letter openers can be used like a clay knife.

Newspapers can be used for armatures and for laying down a barrier when working with water-based clays.

Now go to the garage:

Fishing line can be used as a clay cutter.

Pieces of wood are used for armatures or a surface for mounting your sculpture. They can also be used to flatten out large areas like a press.

Paintbrushes of any size can be used for painting, texturing, and applying rubbing alcohol to polymer clays. The rubbing alcohol acts like a liquid sandpaper to smooth out fingerprints and other imperfections.

Lastly, look in your bathroom:

Waxed dental floss is another option for a clay-cutting tool.

Dental picks can be used for detailing, scoring, and cutting small pieces of clay for detail work.

Toilet paper rolls can be used for armature.

Be creative with your tools. This list is not conclusive. If you see an object and it looks like it can work, chances are it does work. The next chapter brings some of these tools together for a fun and simple clay project using plasticine, the oil-based clay referred to earlier.

Chapter 5: Making a Simple Figure with Oil-Based Clay

All modelling clays are fun to work with. This chapter focuses on a simple figure using plasticine and **common tools from your home**. Take time to get used to the feel of the oil-based clay. Allow yourself to make mistakes and have fun. This medium is very forgiving. It will not dry out, even if you are working on the piece for a long time. Once you have finished this exercise squish the clay, and begin again.

1. Choose an image or model for the subject, or invent one in your mind.

2. Sketch your figure from many angles. Then add measurements to your sketch. For this exercise, make a 12-inch figure.

3. Use **aluminum foil** to create an armature. Twist sections of foil into arms, legs, torso, and head. You can use leftover **bread ties** to secure the pieces together. Use your measurements to make the figure proportionate. You do not need to wrap the aluminum foil with plastic.

4. Put the armature on a **piece of wood**. You will not be attaching the figure. Use the wood as a clean surface for this exercise.

5. Use a **fishing line or waxed dental floss** to cut slices of the plasticine from the block. Then squeeze the plasticine onto the aluminum armature until the entire figure is covered.

6. Once you have covered the armature with 3/8 inch of plasticine, measure again to make sure your figure is still proportionate.

7. Now you can add and subtract clay as necessary to add details to your figure. Tools to use at this point can include **knives, spoons, forks, kabob spears**, etc. Make sure your figure stays symmetric.

Enjoy the process. Take photos of your work when done to track your progress later. Then you can peel the clay off the armature and begin again. Both clay and armature can be reused many times. As you become more confident in sculpting and modelling with clay begin to try different types of clay. You may also invest in advanced tools. The next chapter will cover different types of tools available.

Chapter 6: Using Advanced Tools for More Complex Projects

This book outlines common household items for beginning tools, but dedicated clay tools are invaluable. They are shaped to fit your hand properly for comfort while working. Many tools have specialized functions for very detailed work. This chapter will cover the various tools available.

1. **Sculpting Table:** These tables look like a tall chair with a turntable mounted on top. This is useful for turning your sculpture while working. It typically is on a wheeled base for easy movement around your studio.

2. **Lazy Susan:** These round platforms spin for easy viewing of all sides of the sculpture. These can be found in many materials. Plastic ones are the most convenient for clay modelling, as they will not pull the moisture from your clay.

3. **Calipers:** These are instruments used for exact measurements of the figure. They look similar to a protractor without the attached

pencil. They can be quite large for measuring body parts.

4. **Stainless Steel, Thick Gauge Pasta Machine:** This is used for rolling out ribbons of clay, mixing colors together, and creating sheets of multiple colors. Industrial grade machines work best.

5. **Texture Plates:** These are plastic plates with textures imprinted. These can be rolled through a pasta maker with the clay to imprint the design. They can also be used with a rolling pin.

6. **Clay Gun:** Similar to a caulking gun or cake-icing pipe, the clay gun extrudes clay designs by forcing clay through a die. The dies can have various shapes and are useful for making detailed objects like leaves and ribbons.

7. **Clay Stamps:** This is similar to press stamps found in children's play dough sets. These stamps make detailed small objects as well. Unlike with the clay gun, you will need to trim excess clay off upon removal from the stamp.

8. **Clay Shapers:** These look like paintbrushes with a silicon tip. They are great for pushing polymer clay.

9. **Steel and Stainless Steel Tools:** There is an assortment of these tools to choose from; spatulas, files, and picks come in all shapes and sizes. These are good for shaping and detail work.

10. **Dentist Picks:** The tools a dentist uses for picking your teeth are excellent tools for working in clay.

11. **Wire End Shapers:** These are tools with wires attached to each end. The wires can be shaped as loops, rectangles, and triangles. This tool is used to remove chunks of clay. They come in micro, small, medium, and large.

12. **Saw Rake:** These are similar to the wire end shapers but they have a sharp saw blade on each shaped end.

13. **Wire Wrinkle Tool:** This is a handle with multiple wires on each end. It is used to texture and create the illusion of wrinkles.

14. **Probe Tool:** This handle has a wire wrinkle on one end and a long needle on the other.

15. **Ribbon Tools:** These are similar to wire end shapers. They are made of hard wood with wire ends. Ribbon tools are used for cutting, scraping, and trimming clay.

16. **Clean up Tools:** These have hardwood handles and very precise metal points used for finishing a piece.

17. **Kemper Wooden Clay Tools:** These come in a variety of shapes and sizes and are used for all aspects of sculpting.

Specialized clay tools can make sculpting in clay easy and fun. These tools range in price. Many can be purchased for a few dollars each. As with any tools, there are high-end pieces as well. Search for artist wholesale stores on-line for great deals on bundles of tools.

Conclusion

Sculpting with clay is fun. With this book and your creativity, it can be affordable too. Look for objects in your home that can be used as tools for sculpting. Once you become familiar with your chosen clay and found tools, consider investing in advanced clay tools. These tools make detail work easier to complete.

Research the best possible deals for clay and tools online and in art supply stores. Weigh the costs of the raw materials versus the cost of finishing the piece. Consider how large your sculpture will be and how long it will take to create. Then you can decide what type of clay to use.

Remember to follow the process outlined in chapter three. This process will help each piece to be successful from the start. It is incredibly important to take frequent breaks while first learning how to sculpt in clay. These breaks allow you to take a fresh look at the piece and identify any problem areas.

Above all, remember that working with clay is a creative process involving all the senses. Enjoy the smell, feel, and sounds of the clay as you work with it.

Allow your eyes to focus on the clay and release tension. If you find yourself stressed while working, take a break. Give yourself the time and patience needed to create a beautiful sculpture or model.

Finally, I'd like to thank you for purchasing this book! If you enjoyed it or found it helpful, I'd greatly appreciate it if you'd take a moment to leave a review on Amazon. Thank you!